A WORKBOOK

30 QUESTIONS

TO **ASK** THE **AKASHIC RECORDS** TO **CHANGE** THE **WORLD**

Lindsay Mann

BY MANN
Hartsdale, NY

For permission requests, write to the author at:
lindsay@heyclarity.com

Lindsay Mann
BY MANN

www.heyclarity.com

30 Questions to Ask the Akashic Records to Change the World / Lindsay Mann. — 1st ed.

ISBN 979-8-9863954-3-2

Dedicated to you and all of your incarnations.

Introduction

The Akashic Records have been a profound source of support in my life. I've gained heightened self-awareness and unshakeable trust in my experiences, closed massive chapters making peace with histories of abuse and violence, and have humbly witnessed tremendous healing in those I've worked with. I love the complex layers of who we are, and I find our existence and the mind-blowing worlds around us infinitely fascinating.

New perspectives and staying open to possibilities can change our entire world. Each of us intended to be here at this time in history, no matter how much our faith gets shaken. We may not be able to wrap our heads around the consciousness of what's being presented to us on a mass scale, but we have the tools and resources to see through it all to clarity.

We are a web of clear channels drawn to the Universal information field, the Akashic Records. So let's envision our highest perspective for our world and project it outward, planting seeds for a creative, adaptable, and sustainable future.

I wrote this book to be a time capsule and a reference you can return to as your life and everything around you unfolds. This is *your* book and the physical documentation of chapters in your Soul's journey brought down from the Universe into material form. I hope it brings you inspiration, solace, strength, and wisdom to carry you forward.

WHO AM I?

Why did my Soul choose to incarnate at this time in history?

A blank space for more notes or sketches of visuals

How can I experience the truest expression of my Soul?

What aspects of this life can help me stay in alignment with my true self?

How can my Soul feel at home anywhere, anytime?

What does my higher self look like? What does my lower self look like?

PAST

What experiences from my past, in this lifetime or previous lifetimes, need to be released? How can I release them?

In what past life was I most impactful to the world? How does that past life shape who I am today?

In what past life was I most destructive to the world? How does that past life shape who I am today?

What are the benefits of any adversity, pain, and suffering I experienced in this life or past lives? How did it grow me?

PRESENT

How can I bring myself into the present moment, instantly?

What is clear about my life right now that I need to bring into my awareness?

What is in my blindspot right now that I need to bring into my awareness?

How can I view and appreciate my life exactly as it is in this moment?

FUTURE

How far into the future can I see? What's the range of my foresight?

What does my future self want me to know about my life right now?

How will the world benefit from my current existence, in the future?

What information can be shared with me now, for my highest good, that can best prepare me for any challenges I might face in the future?

MY GUIDES

Who are my ancestors? What messages do they have for me?

Which Spirit Guides/Angels/Passed-On Loved Ones are currently with me? What messages do they have for me?

Why are we together? Why did we choose each other?

How can I connect and communicate with my guides whenever I need them?

MICRO WORLD

What is flowing easily and effortlessly in my life?

What blocks are present in my life? How can I move or shift them?

What outdated stories or patterns are playing on repeat in my life that need to evolve? What new stories or patterns can replace them?

How can I create beneficial impact in my immediate environment for the greatest good of everyone in it?

MACRO WORLD

How can I bring peace to my lineage – past, present, and future?

What can I do or be to best serve the world in this lifetime?

What can I do or be with the greatest of ease to have the most significant impact in the world in this lifetime?

What is my highest vision for the world?

How will I impact the world in this lifetime?

Space for your own questions

Space for sketches of visuals

www.ingramcontent.com/pod-product-compliance
Lightning Source LLC
Chambersburg PA
CBHW070443130626
46553CB00006B/2281